THE WONDERFUL WORLD OF WORDS

10

The Queen's Soldiers

Dr Lubna Alsagoff

PhD Linguistics (Stanford)

Marshall Cavendish
Children

Very well, your Majesty. We will do as you command.

You must keep fit. You must train because you never know when we will need to defend WOW!

The queen realised that there was very little space in WOW castle for them to train!

And the soldiers, true to their word, tried to train. But soon, they were jumping and bumping into one another.

3

5

The queen was very happy to see the soldiers training.

She saw the soldiers _ _ _ . c r e a

She saw the soldiers _ _ _ _ . m u j p

She watched the soldiers _ _ _ _ _ . m c i l p

She saw the soldiers _ _ _ _ _. l a r w c

And later that night, the queen saw the soldiers _ _ _ a wonderful meal. e t a

And then she saw them all go to _ _ _ _ _ _. l e p s e

The camp had a wonderful training course.

You must w _ l _ down a hill.

You must climb up a rope and s _ i _ _ down quickly.

You must _ _ ve some heavy rocks to clear the way.

You must w _ d _ across a pond.

You must _ _ _ g the bell when you are done.

You must _ u _ as fast you as can across the field.

You must w_ _ g_le through the tunnel.

The queen also needed
to see that the soldiers
could do things by themselves.

The soldier run .

The queen also needed to see that the soldiers could do things together.

The soldiers run.

The soldier jump s.

The soldier s jump.

The soldier crawl**s**.

The soldier **s** crawl.

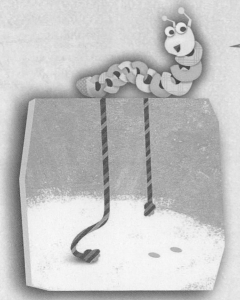

Can you match the verb to the picture?

play

The soldiers _____ up a rope.

drives

The admiral _____ a boat.

climb

The queen _____ a racing car.

rows

The prince and princess _____ the piano.

eats

clean

love

walks

The people _____ the king.

The king _____ in the garden.

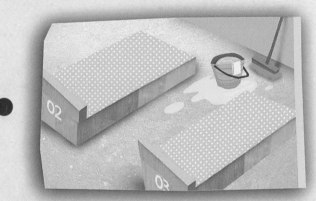

The soldiers _____ their room.

The anteater _____ ants.

The princess was very worried about Donkey.

16

They told her about the strange purple cloud, and how it made the animals sick.

18

19

20

Dear Parents,

In this issue, children should notice and learn:

- When the noun is singular, the verbs take an *s*

- When the noun is plural, and has a *s* ending, the verb has no ending.
  - singular nouns have verbs with *s* endings.
  - plural nouns have verbs with no *s* endings.

- Different plurals that nouns have.

When they read, have them notice this pattern.
This will help them learn subject-verb agreement rules.

Page	Possible Answers
6-7	race | jump | climb | crawl | eat | sleep
8-9	walk | slide | move | wade | wriggle | run | ring
14-15	The soldiers **climb** up a rope. The admiral **rows** a boat. The queen **drives** a racing car. The prince and princess **play** the piano. The people **love** the king. The king **walks** in the garden. The soldiers **clean** their room. The anteater **eats** ants.